D1712661

SOLVING SCIENCE MYSTERIES

Why Do Shadows Lengthen?

All About Light

Nicolas Brasch

PowerKiDS press.
New York

Published in 2010 by The Rosen Publishing Group, Inc.
29 East 21st Street, New York, NY 10010

Produced and designed by Denise Ryan & Associates
Editors: Helen Moore and Edwina Hamilton
Designer: Anita Adams
Photographer: Lyz Turner-Clark
U.S. Editor: Joanne Randolph

Photo Credits: p. 4 bottom: Gavin Spencer; p. 5 top: © Photographer: Jeff Clow | Agency: Dreamstime.com; p. 5 middle: © Photographer: Christophe Testi | Agency: Dreamstime.com; p. 7 top: Ulf Hinze; p. 8: © Photographer:Michael Levy | Agency: Dreamstime.com; p. 9: Paweł Zawistowski; p. 10: James Dare; p. 11 bottom: © Photographer:Ye Liew | Agency: Dreamstime.com; p. 12 top NASA; p. 12 bottom: © Photographer: Andrey Sobolev | Agency: Dreamstime.com; p. 13 top: Julie de Leseleuc; p. 14 bottom left: Fabienne Price; p. 14 bottom right: © Photographer: Casey Bishop | Agency: Dreamstime.com; p. 15 top: © Photographer: Keith Frith | Agency: Dreamstime.com; p. 15 bottom and 18: Photolibrary; p. 17 bottom: Richard Sweet; p. 19 Astrolab; p. 22 © www.iStockphoto.com/Greg Cooksey.

Library of Congress Cataloging-in-Publication Data

Brasch, Nicolas.
 Why do shadows lengthen? : all about light / Nicolas Brasch.
     p. cm. — (Solving science mysteries)
 Includes index.
 ISBN 978-1-61531-891-9 (lib. bdg.) — ISBN 978-1-61531-913-8 (pbk.) —
ISBN 978-1-61531-914-5 (6-pack)
1. Light—Wave-length—Miscellanea—Juvenile literature. 2. Light, Wave theory of—Miscellanea—Juvenile literature. I. Title.
 QC455.B63 2010
 535—dc22

                              2009034094

Manufactured in the United States of America

CPSIA Compliance Information: Batch #WW10PK: For Further Information contact Rosen Publishing, New York, New York at 1-800-237-9932

Contents

Questions About Light and Darkness

Q: What is light?

A: Light is a type of energy that enables things to be seen. Light travels in waves. These waves are known as **electromagnetic** waves because light consists of electrical energy and magnetic energy. Most of the natural light on Earth comes from the Sun. It is created by the Sun burning **hydrogen** at an extremely high temperature.

Q: Why do shadows change?

A: Shadows change their length and direction depending on the position of the Sun. A shadow is longer at the beginning and end of the day, when the Sun is low in the sky, than it is in the middle of the day when the Sun is high overhead. This is because the light hits an object at a low **angle**.

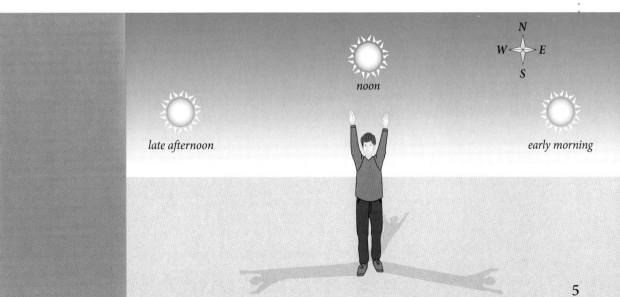

noon

N
W ✧ E
S

late afternoon

early morning

Q: What is white light?

A: Light is made up of many different colors. White is not a color. So how can some light or a color appear to be white? White light is created when all the primary colors in light—green, red, and blue are mixed together equally.

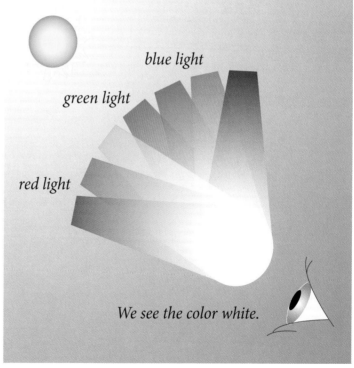

blue light

green light

red light

We see the color white.

Q: What is a polar night?

A: A polar night is when the Sun does not rise above the horizon in a particular place. This **phenomenon** occurs because of the way Earth is tilted at this time. Some places do not receive any sunlight at all and the others receive very little sunlight. The most extreme examples of a polar night are the North Pole and South Pole, which are in darkness for six months of the year.

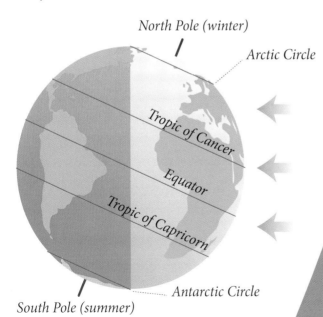

North Pole (winter)

Arctic Circle

Tropic of Cancer

Equator

Tropic of Capricorn

Antarctic Circle

South Pole (summer)

Telling the Time

A sundial is an ancient instrument used to tell the time. It is divided into sections like a clock. In the middle of a sundial is a stick-like object known as a gnomon. The gnomon casts a shadow. The direction of the shadow depends on the position of the Sun. When the Sun is directly above the sundial, the stick does not cast a shadow. At all other times of the day, the gnomon's shadow points to a mark on the sundial that tells us the time.

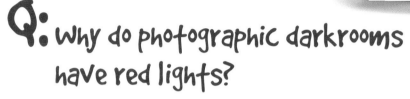

Questions About Light and Color

Q: Why do photographic darkrooms have red lights?

A: Some photographers use film in their cameras and take black and white photographs. They then **develop** the film in darkrooms. The photographic paper that is used to process these photographs is very sensitive to blue and green light. White light contains green and blue, so photographers use red light globes to light their darkrooms. Color processing paper is sensitive to all colors, so developing color photographs has to be done in complete darkness. The red light in darkrooms is known as a safe light.

Q: Why are tomatoes red?

A: Tomatoes contain a **pigment** called lycopene. When the sunlight hits a tomato, the lycopene absorbs all of the colors in the sunlight except for one: red. It reflects the red color, so when you look at a tomato, you see the red being reflected into your eyes. You cannot see the other colors because the lycopene has absorbed them. Unripe tomatoes are in the process of forming lycopene, which is why they are not red.

Questions About Light and Reflections

Q: How do periscopes work?

A: Periscopes are used to see objects from a hidden position. They are most commonly used on submarines. They work through the use of mirrors within a tube. A mirror set at a 45° angle towards the top of the tube will direct an image down the tube to another mirror set at a 45° angle. This mirror directs the image into the eyes of the viewer.

external view of a periscope

how light travels through a periscope

mirror

light →

45°

45°

mirror

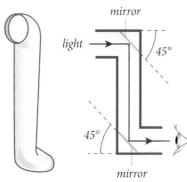

submarine with a periscope

Q: Why do objects in water look closer than they really are?

A: Objects in water look closer than they really are because of a process known as refraction. Refraction is the bending of light as it passes from one medium to another, so when light hits water, it bends. Light reflected off water also bends. It is the bending that takes place as the light leaves the water that causes objects in water to look closer than they really are.

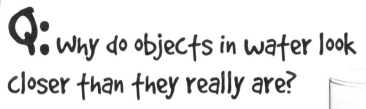

Refraction is making the veins on this leaf look closer than they really are.

It's a Fact

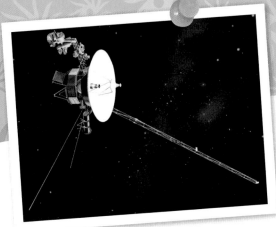

an artist's impression of Voyager 1

> Light Years

A light year is the distance that light can travel in one year. It is equal to about 5.88 trillion miles (9.46 trillion km).

> Distance to the Sun

The Sun is 93 million miles (150 million km) from Earth. It takes just over eight minutes for sunlight to reach Earth.

> A Rainbow Connection

Rainbows are created by sunlight hitting raindrops. The raindrops separate all the colors in the light and reflect them into the air.

> Into the Unknown

The furthest a human-made object has travelled in space is 13 light hours. It took the space probe, *Voyager 1*, 27 years to travel the distance that light would have reached in 13 hours.

> Upside Down

The human eye receives images upside down. The brain turns these images the right way up.

upside down image
of dog on retina

dog

lens

eye

> Moving Images

Movies are not really moving images. They are a collection of still images that are moved across a light source quickly to give the impression of movement. In fact, they are a rapid sequence of photographs.

Color Blindness

Color blindness is the inability to notice a difference between particular colors. The most common type of color blindness is red/green color blindness. More than 10 percent of males are believed to have a form of color blindness. The condition is very rare in females.

Test yourself! Look at the disk on this page. What can you see? If you have red/green blindness you will simply see dots. If not, you will see the number 8.

Can You Believe It?

Solar Power

Sunlight can be converted into electricity. This is because it is a form of energy. When captured by solar **cells**, the energy in the light causes **electrons** to move and create an electric **current**. The electric current can be used to provide lighting, heating, and power to homes and offices.

Impressionism

The art movement known as Impressionism was given this name because painters tried to capture the impression that was created when light shone on what they were painting. Impressionist artists rarely worked indoors. They painted outside.

solar cells in operation on a roof

A price scanner is an example of a laser beam being used.

Laser Beams

A laser beam is a ray of light that has more energy and brightness than a normal ray of light. It is created by changing the electromagnetic waves so they are the same length and remain parallel to each other. This also causes them to be one color, red. The word "laser" stands for "Light Amplification by Stimulated Emission of Radiation."

Who Found Out?

Distance of Earth from the Sun: Aristarchus

The Greek mathematician and astronomer Aristarchus (310 BCE– c. 230 BCE) was the first person to try to calculate the distance between Earth and the Sun. Unfortunately, he was wrong, but his attempt prompted others to try. He also tried to work out the sizes of the Sun and the Moon and the distance between Earth and the Moon. Aristarchus may have been the first person to correctly conclude that the Sun was the center of the solar system.

Electric Light Bulb: Thomas Edison

The American inventor Thomas Edison (1847–1931) created several devices that changed the way light was used. Many of his creations were based on other people's inventions but his **ingenuity** meant that they improved so much that they became affordable and more widely used. Edison developed the electric light bulb and a device that showed moving pictures on a screen. Edison also established an electricity distribution system to light large numbers of houses by electricity.

The Laser:
Charles Townes

The American **physicist** Charles Townes (1915–) shared the 1964 Nobel Prize for Physics for his groundbreaking work in developing the laser. The other winners of the 1964 Nobel Prize for Physics were the Russian physicists Aleksandr Prokhorov and Nikolay Basov.

Townes' work on the laser came after he had developed a maser, a device that emitted **microwaves**. The device, which produced a powerful concentrated form of light, became the laser. Laser light is used in many ways—for eye surgery, 3-D photography, minisubmarines, and price scanners.

The Speed of Light:
Albert Abraham Michelson

The American physicist Albert Abraham Michelson (1852– 1931) was renowned for his work on the measurement of the speed of light. He was born in Strzelno in the Kingdom of Prussia (Poland) and moved to the United States with his parents when he was two years old. While serving as an officer in the U.S. Navy, Michelson started planning a refinement of the rotating mirror methods of Léon Foucault for measuring the speed of light. In 1907 he received the Nobel Prize in Physics, becoming the first American to be awarded the Nobel Prize in sciences.

It's Quiz Time!

The pages where you can find the answers are shown in the red circles.

Find the odd one out

1. green	yellow	red	blue	⑥
2. Arctic Circle	Antarctica	Equator	North Pole	⑦
3. Charles Townes	Aristarchus	Aleksandr Prokhorov	Nikolay Basov	⑯

Choose the correct words

1. Light travels in waves known as
   (electrical, electromagnetic, magnetic) waves. ④

2. The pigment in tomatoes that reflects the red
   color is (lychee, enzyme, lycopene). ⑨

3. Objects in the water look closer than they really are
   because of a process known as (refraction, reflection, rejection). ⑪

Complete **these** sentences

1. A shadow is _____ at the beginning of the day than it is in the _____ of the day when the sun is high overhead. ⑤

2. The word "laser" stands for _____ Amplification by Stimulated Emission of _____. ⑮

3. The stick-like object on the sundial is known as a _____. ⑦

4. It takes just _____ minutes for sunlight to reach Earth. ⑫

Try It Out!

Do you remember why shadows change? Go back and read page 5 again. Now let's try these ideas out for ourselves and put science into action!

What You'll Need:

chalk and a friend to help you

1 Choose a safe, sunny spot outside where you will see how shadows change throughout the day. Mark the spot with a large X using your chalk.

2 Stand on the X and have your friend trace your shadow with the chalk. Write the time next to the chalk line. Repeat this step a few times throughout the day. What happened? When was your shadow longest? Was it always pointing in the same direction?

Glossary

angle (ANG-gul) The space between where two surfaces or lines meet.

cells (SELZ) Small devices used to create an electric current.

current (KUR-ent) A flow of electricity.

develop (dih-VEH-lup) To treat photographic film with chemicals so that pictures appear on it.

electromagnetic (ih-lek-troh-mag-NEH-tik) Having a force of magnetism created by a small bit of electricity.

electrons (ih-LEK-tronz) Particles that have a negative charge and that orbit around the nucleus of an atom.

hydrogen (HY-dreh-jen) The most common gas in the universe.

impression (im-PREH-shen) A vague idea.

ingenuity (in-jeh-NOO-uh-tee) Cleverness.

microwaves (MY-kruh-wayvz) Electromagnetic waves with very high frequencies.

periscopes (PER-uh-skohps) Tools that are used to see above the surface of the water from below the surface.

phenomenon (fih-NO-meh-non) An occurrence or happening.

physicist (FIH-zuh-sist) Someone who studies physics (the way things act and react).

pigment (PIG-ment) A colored substance.

sequence (SEE-kwens) A series in the order of the way things happen.

Index

Web Sites

Due to the changing nature of Internet links, PowerKids Press has developed an online list of Web sites related to the subject of this book. This site is updated regularly. Please use this link to access the list: *www.powerkidslinks.com/ssm/length/*